For My Wife
ANNIE

STERLING CHILDREN'S BOOKS
New York

An Imprint of Sterling Publishing Co., Inc.
1166 Avenue of the Americas
New York, NY 10036

ISBN 978-1-4549-2360-2

Distributed in Canada by Sterling Publishing Co., Inc.
c/o Canadian Manda Group, 664 Annette Street, Toronto, Ontario M6S 2C8, Canada
Distributed in the United Kingdom by GMC Distribution Services, Castle Place, 166 High Street,
Lewes, East Sussex BN7 1XU, England. Distributed in Australia by NewSouth Books,
45 Beach Street, Coogee, NSW 2034, Australia

For information about custom editions, special sales, and premium and corporate
purchases, please contact Sterling Special Sales at 800-805-5489
or specialsales@sterlingpublishing.com.

Manufactured in China

Lot #:
2 4 6 8 10 9 7 5 3 1
05/18

sterlingpublishing.com

Design by Jason Henry and Irene Vandervoort
The artwork for this book
was created digitally.

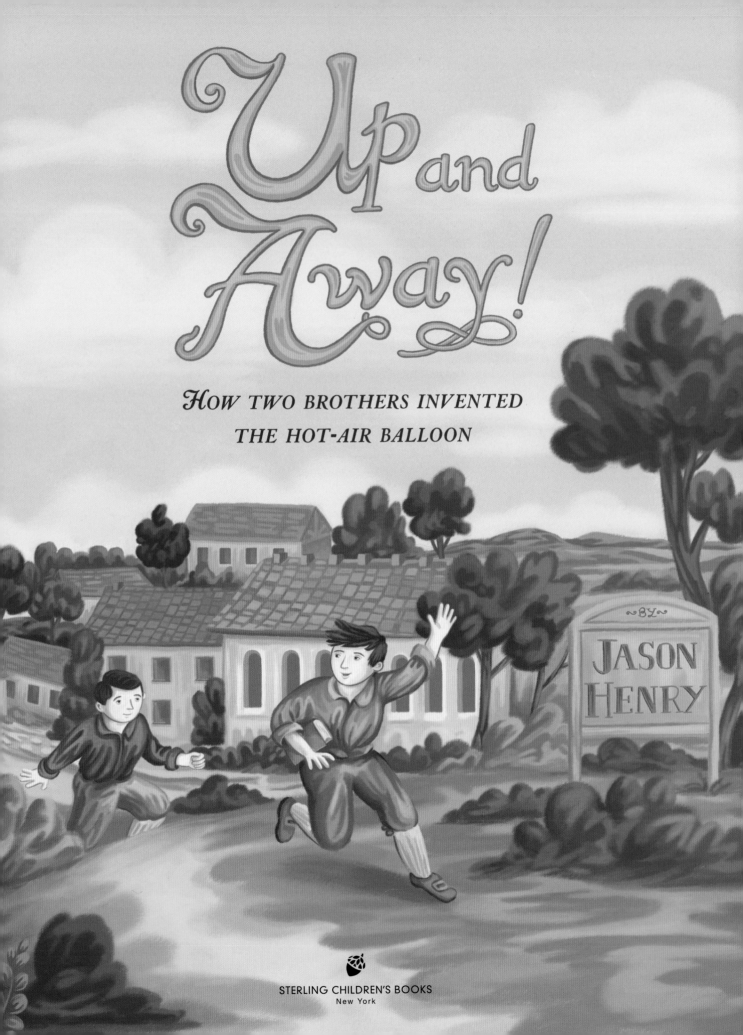

Up and Away!

How Two Brothers Invented the Hot-Air Balloon

STERLING CHILDREN'S BOOKS
New York

Joseph-Michel Montgolfier was a dreamer, just like you.

Even at a young age, Joseph was curious to know how everything worked. Growing up in Annonay, France, in the mid-1700s, he flew kites, wondering how they stayed aloft like the great eagles in the sky. He took apart clocks and machines in his family's home to see what made them tick.

As he grew older, Joseph read piles of books about math and science. He loved those subjects because through them he learned how the world worked. Joseph applied that knowledge to build amazing things. He wanted to be known as a great inventor, so he continued to read, learn, and experiment as much as he could.

Of the sixteen Montgolfier children, Joseph was closest to his brother Jacques-Étienne. Étienne was not a dreamer like Joseph. He was the opposite—practical, matter-of-fact, and good at business. Even though their personalities were different, the brothers shared a common interest in science and the latest technical innovations of the day.

When their father asked Étienne to manage the family's papermaking factory, it was a natural fit. Joseph was happy for his brother, as he preferred to spend time with his books, thinking of possibilities for his inventions.

One afternoon, Joseph stretched and decided to take a break from a very long morning of study. Lost in thought, he walked out the front door, forgetting to close it behind him.

A gust of wind blew through the open doorway. Joseph's papers looped up into the air. Many landed in the fireplace.

Joseph returned home to a big mess, then looked over at the fireplace. Such a lot of work, gone so quickly!

As he sat and watched bits of paper crackle and rise in the smoke of the fireplace, a thought came to him—and, oh, what a thought!

Joseph asked himself: what caused those bits of paper to rise in the fireplace? *Something* must lift them into the air.

At this time in history, discoveries were being made in a new science called chemistry. Oxygen and hydrogen had been discovered a few years earlier, and hydrogen was now known to be lighter than air. Could it be possible there was a *new* gas within the smoke and fire that also had lifting properties?

After observing the fire further, Joseph thought it must be so. More ideas rushed through his mind. If enough gas were contained in a large vessel, it would surely lift itself into the air. He could build a flying machine!

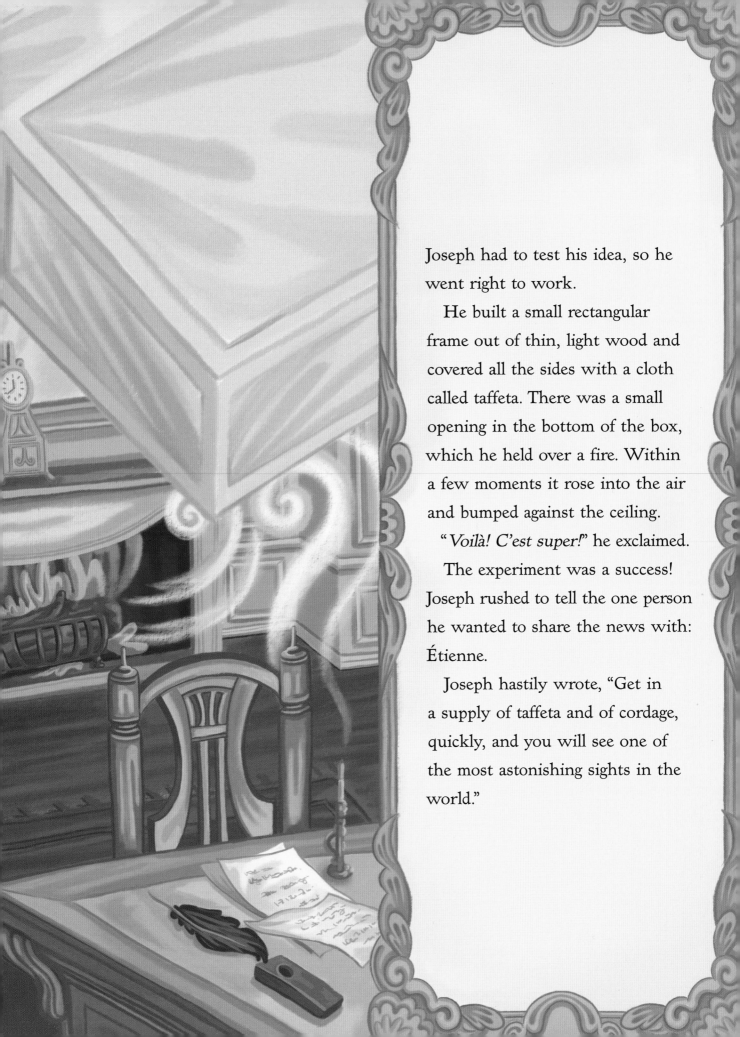

Joseph had to test his idea, so he went right to work.

He built a small rectangular frame out of thin, light wood and covered all the sides with a cloth called taffeta. There was a small opening in the bottom of the box, which he held over a fire. Within a few moments it rose into the air and bumped against the ceiling.

"*Voilà! C'est super!*" he exclaimed.

The experiment was a success! Joseph rushed to tell the one person he wanted to share the news with: Étienne.

Joseph hastily wrote, "Get in a supply of taffeta and of cordage, quickly, and you will see one of the most astonishing sights in the world."

It was not like Étienne to be caught up in one of his brother's wild endeavors, but after seeing Joseph's experiment for himself, he knew that the discovery was an amazing one.

Together, the brothers designed and built a large sphere, three times the size of the small box Joseph had used in his first experiment. They realized that the larger the object was, the larger the heat source would need to be to fuel it. A blazing fire was placed under the open end of the fabric, filling it with heat and billows of smoke. As it expanded, the sphere strained at the ropes and broke away!

It floated out of sight . . . landing dramatically in a neighbor's field.

Talk spread across the countryside of strange things happening at the Montgolfiers' home. Étienne knew it wouldn't be long before others figured out that the brothers were constructing a flying machine.

Concerned that someone else would take the idea and claim it as his own, Étienne acted quickly and prepared for a public demonstration in the town square. There, everyone, including the town officials, would see that the Montgolfiers had invented the world's first flying machine.

On a damp June day, Joseph and Étienne brought an enormous sphere—which they now called an aerostat—to the town square. Along with a team of men, they built another hot and smoky fire beneath the mass of cloth. They even burned old shoes and wool to get the fire roaring. The aerostat filled quickly. Shouts arose from the crowd. The balloon was released into the sky, reaching a height of about three thousand feet before slowly descending.

No one had seen anything like it before.

The town officials wrote about the flight in their official ledgers, recording the date of June 4, 1783. Now, for all time, it would be known that the invention that flew on this date was the work of the Montgolfier brothers.

News of the aerostat spread quickly through academic circles in Paris and Lyon via newspaper reports and word of mouth—and even reached the ear of the king of France! King Louis XVI wanted to see the aerostat for himself. He loved inventions, and thought this one was so important that not only he should witness it but all of France, too.

His invitation was a great honor. Joseph and Étienne were determined to impress him.

They asked themselves: should they be the ones to fly in their invention in front of the king? No person had ever traveled into the sky before—and their father had begged them to never fly because he feared for their safety. Who, then, should they send aloft?

Being the scientists that they were, the brothers chose to send three animals that would almost surely survive a brief journey into the sky. A rooster and duck would be fine choices, since they were birds. A third passenger, a sheep, was also chosen because it was hardy and about the weight of a small man. When the three animals landed safely, the brothers figured, it would be much easier for people to follow suit.

Upon their arrival in Paris, Joseph and Étienne visited the workshop of Jean-Baptiste Réveillon, a friend of Étienne's from their school days. Réveillon was known for making the most beautiful wallpaper in France.

The designs Réveillon had on display in his workshop inspired the brothers.
He collaborated with them and used his patterns to decorate the aerostat in a way
that would be worthy of royalty; they would dazzle all of France.

Réveillon decorated the aerostat with beautiful blue-and-gold emblems showing the king's royal signature. The new aerostat took a total of four months to construct.

Outside the workshop, the aerostat was tethered to two tall poles, and a large brazier of burning straw and wood was placed underneath it. Slowly, the massive machine filled and took shape. It lifted and strained at the ropes until the skies opened up and rain began to pour down. The fire in the brazier went out. The intricate designs Réveillon had painted on the outside of the aerostat cracked and peeled off in soggy, curled sheets that fell to the ground.

Months of work had been destroyed by one sudden rainstorm, and the king was expecting a demonstration in a few short weeks!

Disappointing the king was not an option. The brothers had no choice but to begin repairing the aerostat quickly. What originally took them months to build, they restored in just four days.

When it came time to test the new aerostat, the skies were clear. The three friends gazed up at what they had created, and the possibilities ahead of them seemed infinite.

On September 19, 1783, thousands of French citizens gathered in the courtyard of the king's palace in Versailles to witness the historic flight. Underneath the large platform in the center of the courtyard, the Montgolfiers began to inflate the aerostat. A curtain off to the side then opened, and two

figures walked over to Étienne—King Louis and Queen Marie Antoinette!

King Louis asked, "Monsieur Montgolfier, surely will you tell me
how this all works?"

And he did.

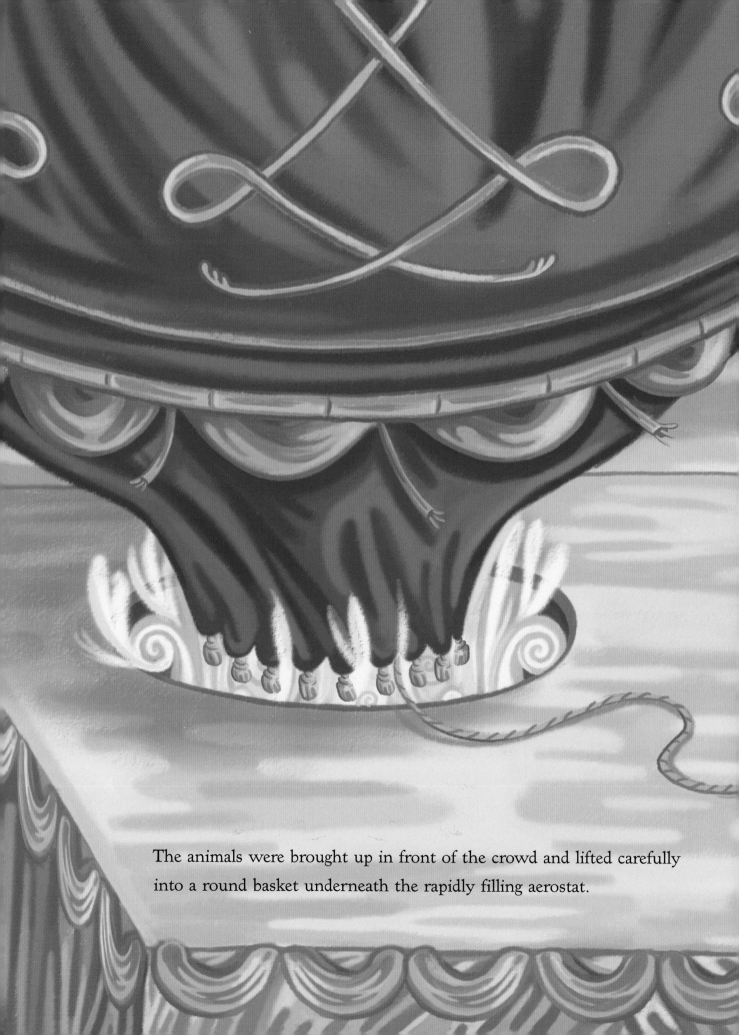

The animals were brought up in front of the crowd and lifted carefully into a round basket underneath the rapidly filling aerostat.

The balloon strained at its ropes and was let loose into the sky. The crowd cheered wildly.

Everyone watched in amazement as the balloon
soared over their heads and out of sight.

The king's horsemen tracked the balloon's progress as it traveled across the countryside. They had to gallop to keep up with it.

After two miles, the aerostat began to lose the hot air trapped within it, and it slowly descended into a forest meadow.

Happy to be on the ground once again, the sheep bolted out of the basket and began grazing on the soft grass. The duck and rooster squawked and flapped their wings.

The king's horsemen soon caught up with the first aeronauts and carried them back in honor to the palace.

News of the Montgolfiers' incredible flight at Versailles traveled quickly, first across Europe, and then overseas. The entire world became dreamers, too.

Author's Note

It's amazing to think that an observation of something as ordinary as fire could lead Joseph and Étienne to create the first successful flying machine. There are many stories throughout history about what actually sparked Joseph's idea—some accounts say he was inspired by watching a wet shirt dry over the heat of a fire or by staring into a fireplace as he contemplated a military battle. We don't know what actually went through Joseph's mind, but in order to tell his story, I used the common theme from the various theories—observation of a fire—to show how Joseph's curiosity led to his experiments with ballooning.

You might be wondering what happened after the astounding flight at Versailles. What of our intrepid animal aeronauts? The three heroes lived the rest of their days in the king's palace as part of his menagerie, home to his collection of prize animals from across the globe. As for Étienne and Joseph, they quickly became two of the most celebrated people in all of Europe. Images of colorful aerostats adorned much of the merchandise and fashion of the day, resulting in a period of "balloonomania" in the late eighteenth and early nineteenth centuries.

The world couldn't wait to see what was next from the Montgolfiers.

On November 21, 1783, just a few months after the Versailles flight, the brothers prepared to test a new aerostat (now called a *montgolfière* in honor of its inventors). This one was even larger than the last. It was seventy feet high and held fifty percent more air than the Versailles balloon. Instead of being inflated on the ground with a limited amount of hot air, it would carry a brazier aboard, so the balloon could travel with its own heat source and be re-inflated as needed. This balloon was built with a specific purpose in mind—to carry the first humans into the sky.

Two men volunteered to be the crew on this airship: science teacher and adventurer Jean-François Pilâtre de Rozier and nobleman François Laurent, the marquis d'Arlandes. As the new aerostat rose above the crowd and buildings, Pilâtre waved his handkerchief, and d'Arlandes began stoking the fire on board with bales of straw. The balloon floated toward the center of Paris, sailing over Nôtre-Dame and Saint-Sulpice. After about twenty-five minutes, the two men landed it safely in farmland just outside the city.

One witness to this flight, Benjamin Franklin, wrote of the craft in his journal and signed a document certifying the event. When someone asked Franklin what use this invention was, he responded, "What use is a newborn baby?" True to that, these early flights were the fuel to a new age of invention and innovation—for this was the birth of the age of flight.

Bibliography

Alfred, Randy. "March 21, 1999: Around the World in 20 Days." *Wired.com*, March 21, 2008. https://www.wired.com/2008/03/dayintech-0321/.

BBC News, "Solar Impulse Completes Historic Round-the-World Trip," BBC.com, July 26, 2016, http://www.bbc.com/news/science-environment-36890563.

Bonafoux, Pascal, and Gilles Targat. *Behind the Scenes in Versailles*. Paris, France: Hachette Livre, 2009.

Browne, Malcolm W. "Balloon History, and in Only 20 Days." *NYTimes.com*, March 21, 1999. http://www.nytimes.com/1999/03/21/world/balloon-history-and-in-only-20-days.html.

Darling, David. *The Rocket Man: And Other Extraordinary Characters in the History of Flight*. London, UK: Oneworld, 2013.

Ehrenfried, Manfred. *Stratonauts: Pioneers Venturing into the Stratosphere*. New York: Springer Praxis Books, 2014.

Encyclopaedia Brittanica, eds. "Joseph-Michel and Jacques-Étienne Montgolfier." *Brittanica.com*, accessed January 15, 2018. https://www.britannica.com/biography/Montgolfier-brothers.

Gillispie, Charles Coulston. *The Montgolfier Brothers and the Invention of Aviation 1783–1784*. Princeton, NJ: Princeton Legacy Library, 2014.

"Gondola, Breitling Orbiter 3." Smithsonian National Air and Space Museum, accessed January 15, 2018. https://airandspace.si.edu/collection-objects/gondola-breitling-orbiter-3.

"Gordon Bennett Cup (Ballooning)." IPFS.io, accessed January 15, 2018. https://ipfs.io/ipfs/QmXoypizjW3WknFiJnKLwHCnL72vedxjQkDDP1mXWo6uco/wiki/Gordon_Bennett_Cup_in_ballooning.html.

Holmes, Richard. *Falling Upwards: How We Took to the Air*. New York: Pantheon, 2013.

HowStuffWorks. Podcast. *The Montgolfier Brothers and Their Balloons*, September 7, 2016. https://www.missedinhistory.com/podcasts/montgolfier-brothers.htm.

Kennedy, Gregory P. "America's First Flight." StratoCat.com, November 24, 2016. http://stratocat.com.ar/artics/blanchard-e.htm.

"The Montgolfiers Fly at Annonay." HistoricWings.com, June 4, 2012. http://fly.historicwings.com/2012/06/the-montgolfiers-fly-at-annonay/.

NASA, ed. "First Shuttle Launch." NASA.gov, last modified August 7, 2017. https://www.nasa.gov/multimedia/imagegallery/image_feature_2488.html.

"October 14, 1947: Yeager Breaks Sound Barrier." History.com, accessed January 15, 2018. http://www.history.com/this-day-in-history/yeager-breaks-sound-barrier.

Sharp, Tim. "The First Hot-Air Balloon: The Greatest Moments in Flight." *Space.com*, July 16, 2012. https://www.space.com/16595-montgolfiers-first-balloon-flight.html.

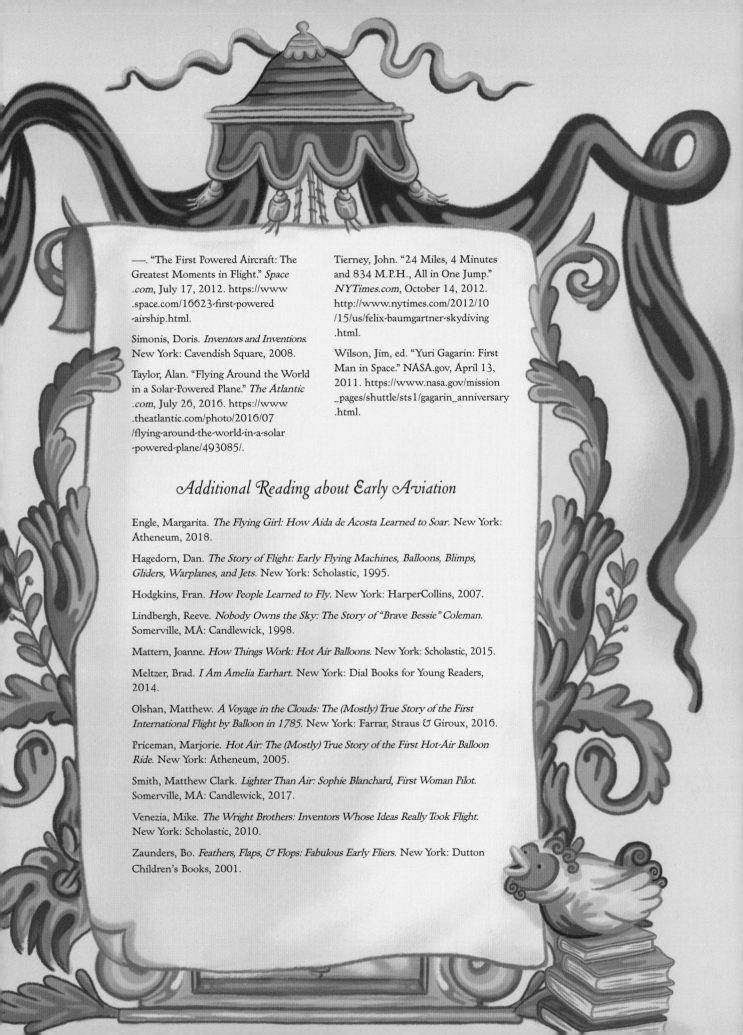

——. "The First Powered Aircraft: The Greatest Moments in Flight." *Space .com*, July 17, 2012. https://www .space.com/16623-first-powered -airship.html.

Simonis, Doris. *Inventors and Inventions*. New York: Cavendish Square, 2008.

Taylor, Alan. "Flying Around the World in a Solar-Powered Plane." *The Atlantic .com*, July 26, 2016. https://www .theatlantic.com/photo/2016/07 /flying-around-the-world-in-a-solar -powered-plane/493085/.

Tierney, John. "24 Miles, 4 Minutes and 834 M.P.H., All in One Jump." *NYTimes.com*, October 14, 2012. http://www.nytimes.com/2012/10 /15/us/felix-baumgartner-skydiving .html.

Wilson, Jim, ed. "Yuri Gagarin: First Man in Space." NASA.gov, April 13, 2011. https://www.nasa.gov/mission _pages/shuttle/sts1/gagarin_anniversary .html.

Additional Reading about Early Aviation

Engle, Margarita. *The Flying Girl: How Aida de Acosta Learned to Soar*. New York: Atheneum, 2018.

Hagedorn, Dan. *The Story of Flight: Early Flying Machines, Balloons, Blimps, Gliders, Warplanes, and Jets*. New York: Scholastic, 1995.

Hodgkins, Fran. *How People Learned to Fly*. New York: HarperCollins, 2007.

Lindbergh, Reeve. *Nobody Owns the Sky: The Story of "Brave Bessie" Coleman*. Somerville, MA: Candlewick, 1998.

Mattern, Joanne. *How Things Work: Hot Air Balloons*. New York: Scholastic, 2015.

Meltzer, Brad. *I Am Amelia Earhart*. New York: Dial Books for Young Readers, 2014.

Olshan, Matthew. *A Voyage in the Clouds: The (Mostly) True Story of the First International Flight by Balloon in 1785*. New York: Farrar, Straus & Giroux, 2016.

Priceman, Marjorie. *Hot Air: The (Mostly) True Story of the First Hot-Air Balloon Ride*. New York: Atheneum, 2005.

Smith, Matthew Clark. *Lighter Than Air: Sophie Blanchard, First Woman Pilot*. Somerville, MA: Candlewick, 2017.

Venezia, Mike. *The Wright Brothers: Inventors Whose Ideas Really Took Flight*. New York: Scholastic, 2010.

Zaunders, Bo. *Feathers, Flaps, & Flops: Fabulous Early Fliers*. New York: Dutton Children's Books, 2001.

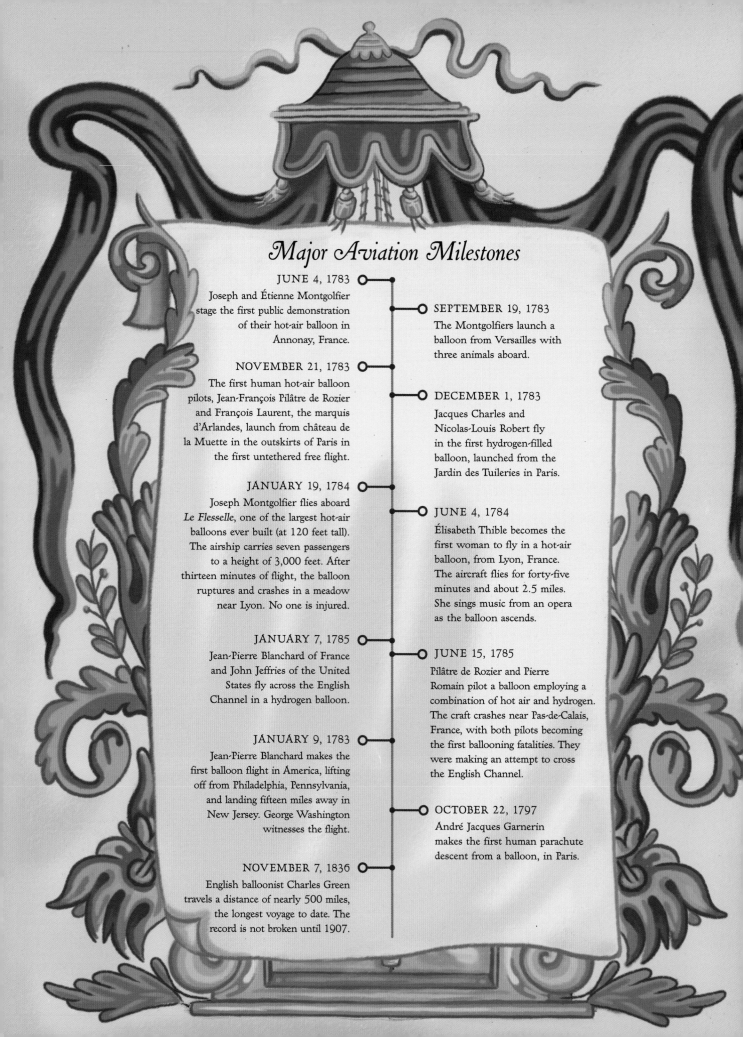

Major Aviation Milestones

JUNE 4, 1783

Joseph and Étienne Montgolfier stage the first public demonstration of their hot-air balloon in Annonay, France.

SEPTEMBER 19, 1783

The Montgolfiers launch a balloon from Versailles with three animals aboard.

NOVEMBER 21, 1783

The first human hot-air balloon pilots, Jean-François Pilâtre de Rozier and François Laurent, the marquis d'Arlandes, launch from château de la Muette in the outskirts of Paris in the first untethered free flight.

DECEMBER 1, 1783

Jacques Charles and Nicolas-Louis Robert fly in the first hydrogen-filled balloon, launched from the Jardin des Tuileries in Paris.

JANUARY 19, 1784

Joseph Montgolfier flies aboard *Le Flesselle*, one of the largest hot-air balloons ever built (at 120 feet tall). The airship carries seven passengers to a height of 3,000 feet. After thirteen minutes of flight, the balloon ruptures and crashes in a meadow near Lyon. No one is injured.

JUNE 4, 1784

Élisabeth Thible becomes the first woman to fly in a hot-air balloon, from Lyon, France. The aircraft flies for forty-five minutes and about 2.5 miles. She sings music from an opera as the balloon ascends.

JANUARY 7, 1785

Jean-Pierre Blanchard of France and John Jeffries of the United States fly across the English Channel in a hydrogen balloon.

JUNE 15, 1785

Pilâtre de Rozier and Pierre Romain pilot a balloon employing a combination of hot air and hydrogen. The craft crashes near Pas-de-Calais, France, with both pilots becoming the first ballooning fatalities. They were making an attempt to cross the English Channel.

JANUARY 9, 1783

Jean-Pierre Blanchard makes the first balloon flight in America, lifting off from Philadelphia, Pennsylvania, and landing fifteen miles away in New Jersey. George Washington witnesses the flight.

OCTOBER 22, 1797

André Jacques Garnerin makes the first human parachute descent from a balloon, in Paris.

NOVEMBER 7, 1836

English balloonist Charles Green travels a distance of nearly 500 miles, the longest voyage to date. The record is not broken until 1907.